INTRODUCTION

My little homemade chutney and jams business started from simple roots, the love of cooking for family and friends. I have always enjoyed cooking and my family and friends suggested that I branch out and share my products with other people.

I am passionate about cooking with as few ingredients as possible and a lot of my fruit and vegetables are grown in my allotment or given to me by the same family and friends, I originally created my jams for. Most of my products are suitable for vegetarians and vegans. I also have a range of gluten free products. I am passionate about caring for the environment and try and recycle or reuse as much of my packaging as possible.

All of my products are created with love and passion in my own kitchen and I hope you get as much joy from them as I do.

Tricia Sweet

Easy Jam And Chutney Recipes

TRICIA SWEET

First Printing: May 2021

Published by: Little Nell Publishing at The Old Curiosity Bookshop, 115 Loughborough Road, Hathern, Leicestershire LE12 5HZ

www.oldcuriositybookshop.co.uk.com

A copy of this book has been deposited with the British Library according to the Legal deposit Libraries Act 2003 and has been sent to: Legal Deposit Office, The British Library, Boston Spa, Wetherby, West Yorkshire LS23 7BY.

Additional copies will be sent to Bodleian Libraries University of Oxford, Cambridge University Library, the National Library of Scotland, the National Library of Wales and the Library of Trinity College Dublin on their request.

ISBN: 9798749904758

CONTENTS

ACKNOWLEDGMENTS

I would like to say that writing this book has been a big achievement for me as I am severely dyslexic and never dreamt that I would ever write a book, but thank you to my lovely friend Tina who owns the Old Curiosity Bookshop in Hathern, who has encouraged me to slowly write this book one page at a time over a year.

Another big thank you to my three daughters Emma, Rachel and Phillippa, for being supportive and encouraging me to set up my own business and write this book also.

Further thanks must go to my adopted Dad, Mr Brian Dixon for helping me set up market stalls in the cold and the rain and for believing in me and helping me find retail outlets to sell my products.

I would just like also like to mention some of the places that have now been selling my jams and chutneys for over a year:

- The Old Curiosity Bookshop in Hathern
- Elms Farm in Costock
- Stevens Lane Farm Shop in Breaston
- The Veg Pact in Draycot
- The Scoff and Shop in Ticknall

1 BACKGROUND

Myself as a child I always loved to be in the kitchen cooking and used to cook with my mother and father all different types of recipes. However, we never had a lot of money, so a lot of the food we cooked was good old-fashioned cheap food which actually was very good for you like large pans of soups and stews which we would sometimes have for three or four day in a row.

I can remember my father teaching me how to cook Yorkshire puddings and he used to make such a big bowl to feed all seven of us. He would use a good quantity of flour, six eggs, which he would mix together; then slowly add the milk with a pinch of salt and he would always add a tiny bit of water and then let it settle for a good few hours before using.

I also used to love cookery at school, making cakes and pies to bring home for the family to eat. I struggled very much at school but one of the things I excelled at was always cooking. I was also taught to cook the most gorgeous broth which was made from the leftover chicken bones after we had had a Sunday dinner, which would feed our whole family of seven for another meal. On the odd occasion I still do this now as I think it is the best chicken soup you could ever taste.

I started my little jam making hobby on the narrowboat I used to live on, I used to give some of my products to other people that lived on narrowboats. One day I mentioned to a neighbour that I would love to run my own business, she said that my chutneys and jams were great and why didn't I start to sell them. Then family and friends started saving me all their jars, and then my hobby started to become a small income. As this slowly increased, people got to know more and more about my jams and chutneys.

I got busier as people wanted to buy more products. This is when I came to the realisation that maybe I could turn this into a real business.

With the modern mechanisation processes for supermarkets, preserving became almost a thing of the past as factories could produce the stuff much faster and quicker than what we could in a private kitchen. However, over the years I believe that manufacturers have put a lot of unnecessary artificial flavourings, colourings in a lot of our jams, chutneys, and marmalade. As it is made in large bulk and produced so that we can keep it on our shelves longer.

When you make home-made jam, chutney, or marmalade, you do not need to use any artificial flavourings and colourings and the result is a much nicer tasting product than the products you buy from the shops that are manufactured in automated factories. I passionately believe that this is one of the reasons nowadays that people are suffering from allergies in their diet, as we now use too many artificial products in manufacturing. So I think for this reason that many people are now turning back to the old ways of cooking preserves as when they taste them they know that they get a better quality of food yes a little bit more expensive and time-consuming but in the long run you know exactly what is in the product.

The history of how preserving came about

I would like to explain a little about the of history of preserving foods years ago. When people started to grow and farm their own foods it began became necessary to try and preserve the food they were producing to keep longer as there were no such things as refrigerators in those days. People did not have access to food from around the world until much later in our history. So, this was how preserving fruits and vegetables came about. It was around 10,000 years ago when products such as acids, salts, alcohol, and sugar were discovered to have preservative properties. How this actually worked was not properly understood until around about the 19th century but the fact that they did was all that matters.

During this period, in larger households the mistress or housekeeper would have been in charge of all the preserving of foods that needed to be kept for the household to eat over the winter period. Preserving in those days was a kitchen skill and became second nature to cooks up to a few generations ago. They would have made a selection of jams, chutneys, marmalades, wine, fruit in syrups, pickles, and potted meat.

.

2 EQUIPMENT & USEFUL INFORMATION

A list of essential items that you will need to make jams, marmalades, and chutneys.

A good stainless-steel Preserving pan:

The heavy base of the pan helps with the distribution of heat and the wide sides allow for rapid boiling without splashing.

A jam or sugar thermometer:
Used for giving you accurate setting temperature for jams and marmalades.

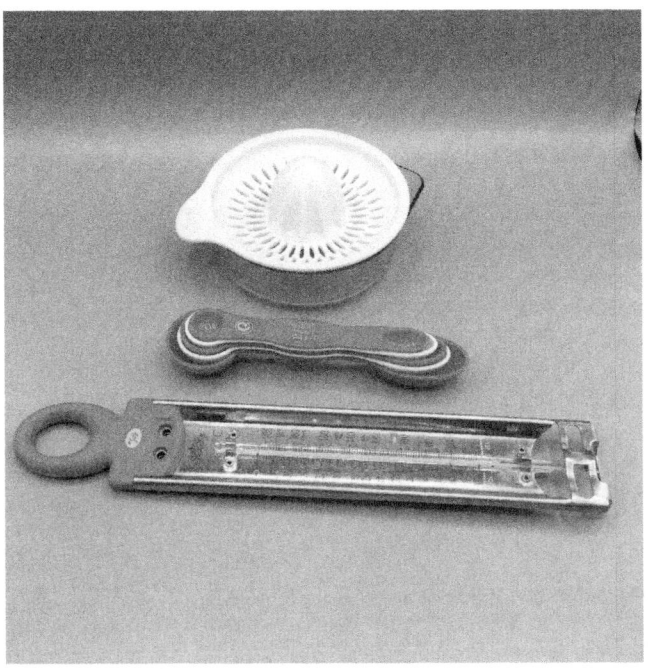

Wooden spoons:
A long-handled spoon is essential for preserving as the mixture is extremely hot and splashes can cause burns.

Muslin squares:
Used in wrapping pipes and all the membrane, and lemon skin for marmalade. Also useful for straining liquid as you make jams or jelly.

Scales:
For measuring ingredients and weighting the amount of jam or chutney in the jar.

Measuring Jugs:
Useful for measuring liquids such as vinegars and water.

Ladle:
A metal ladle is great for putting the hot jam or chutney into the jars and you can also sterilise and wash it well.

Jam Funnel:
This is essential for adding hot jam, marmalade, and chutneys into the jars without spilling the mixture all over the jar or work surface.

Colander: (nylon sieve)

Jam Jars:
You can re-use jars, but you will need to replace the lids. as the rubber seals inside the lid may perish.

Front Labels and Contents Labels

Labelling your product is especially important, then you know exactly what is in the jars for jam, marmalade, or chutney. It is essential for you to put the ingredients on the back because if it is used by someone else, many people have allergies. Also, a use by date is good practise.

Sterilising Jars and Lids

The sterilisation process is particularly important when preserving, whatever type of jar you are using, or all your hard work will be lost if your jam is exposed to contaminants.

Preserving jars can be glass with metal lids the metal lid must have a rubber seal round the edge. You can also you use kilner jars with a washable rubber seal. The seal help to create a vacuum whilst the jars are cooling to keep your products free from contamination.

Always check jars carefully before using for any ridges or chips on the mouth of the jar, as this prevents the lids from giving you an airtight seal. Wash the jars thoroughly in clean soapy water then rinse under cold water to remove any soapsuds, then leave to drain.

There are two ways in which you can sterilise your jars before putting in the jam. You can either boil them in hot water, or I prefer to pop them in the oven for around about 10 minutes on a baking tray, preheat your oven to 170 C fan oven 150 C/ gas mark 3. Do not put your Lids or rubber seals in the oven as the lids will go rusty and the seals will melt. The best way to sterilise the lids, is in a hot boiling pan of water for 10 minutes. I also put my ladle and funnel in to sterilise at the same time, them everything is ready at the same time for jarring your jam or chutneys.

If using recycled jars, just soak them in hot soapy water to remove all the labels and then use the same process as above.

Pectin

The pectin in fruit helps the jam to set. Some fruit are higher in pectin content. some have a medium pectin content, and the others are low in pectin. Try to use fruit when there are dry, fresh, or almost ripe. If the fruit is fresh try to cook the jams the same day as the fruit's pectin starts to decrease over night.

Higher in pectin content:
Cooking apples, blackcurrants, gooseberries, quinces, freshly picked raspberries, damson, some plums, redcurrant, cranberries, and Seville orange, are all high in pectin and great to mix with other fruit or use separately. You should get a good set with these fruits.

Medium in pectin content:
Fresh apricots, early blackberries/brambles, Greengages, lemons, limes, Logan berries and sweet oranges.

Low in pectin content:
Strawberries, grapefruit, tangerines, elderflowers, rhubarb, marrow, medlars, pears and tomatoes.

Mixing ingredients with fruits and vegetables that are high in pectin will help with the setting process for your jams. Also using your own homemade pectin, which is explained further on in the book.

Make your own pectin stock

When using apples for pie and chutney do not throw away the peel, pips, or cores. Also, the skin and pips of lemons, can be kept to make your own pectin. Put in a pan and cover with water, bring to the boil and simmer slowly for 45 minutes. Allow to cool, then pour through a jelly bag or muslin and drain overnight. You can tell if the pectin stock is good by looking and if you can see thickness in the juice. You can freeze in 300ml containers. It ready to then add to any jam needing pectin. Other uses for pectin are mentioned later on.

Testing the Setting Point for Jams.

Time guide from when the sugar has been added and the jam starts a rolling boil, as follows:

After 10 minutes if the fruit is High in pectin content.
After 15 minutes if the fruit has Medium pectin content
After 20 minutes if the fruit is low in pectin content

Keep the preserves off the heat when testing or it may go beyond the setting point. There are three different ways to perform the test. I prefer the plate method below however you can use any of the others if you wish.

1: Put a small plate in the fridge to chill. Then put 1tsp of jam on the plate let it cool briefly then push with your finger if the jam wrinkles, it is ready.

2: Put a jam thermometer into hot water and then put into the jam mixture. If it shows 105 C/220 f then the setting point has been reached.

3: Dip a wooden spoon in the jam. Remove it and twist it a few times to cool the jam. Let if fall off the spoon. If it runs together and forms droplets that hang on the edge of the spoon. It is ready.

Sugars for Jams

I would just like to talk a little bit about sugar. I just use ordinary granulated sugar when making jams, I find this works very well and is a reasonable price. You can buy preserving sugar, but I find this can be very pricey and do not feel it is necessary to use preserving agents in a jam if you cook it in the correct way. Preserving sugar does not produce so much froth on the top of the pan.

Using 60% or higher of sugar is just a strong a preservative as salt is. The salt draws the moisture out of the food as does sugar, the higher the concentrate of sugar the longer you can keep your preserves.

Sugar is mostly used to preserve fruits. But a combination of vinegar and sugar is used with fruit and vegetables for savoury chutneys and relishes. Food usually preserved in sugar are jams, jellies, fruit cheeses, and butter and crystalised fruit. Other sugars that are suitable are cane, granulated cane, sugar beet, and golden finish sugar is also suitable. However dark brown and moist sugars are too strong for Sweet preserving.

Metrication Chart

Spoon measures:

1 tablespoon	15ml approx.
2 teaspoons	10ml approx.
1 teaspoon	5ml approx.
½ teaspoon	2.5ml approx.

Solid measures:

Metric	Imperial
Grams: g	Ounces: (oz)
25g	1oz
50g	2oz
75g	3oz
100g -125g	4oz (¼lb)
150g	5oz
175g	6oz
200g	7oz
225g	8oz (½lb)
250g	9oz
275g	10oz
300g	11oz
350g	12oz (¾lb)
375g	13oz
400g	14oz
425g	15oz
450g	16oz

1,000g = 1 Kilogram
Both measurement weights are an approximate evaluation. From Imperial to metric it is rounded down to the nearest 25 g. 28.32 g is the exact conversion of 1 ounce

1kg 360g	Approximately 1.35kg	3lb
1kg 818g	Approximately 1.75kg	4lb
2kg 270g	Approximately 2.25kg	5lb
2kg 720g	Approximately 2.75kg	6lb
3kg 175g	Approximately 3.20kg	7lb
3kg 630g	Approximately 3.35kg	8lb
4kg 80g	Approximately 4.75kg	9lb
4kg 535g	Approximately 4.50kg	10lb

Temperature Chart guide

(as myself personally I still use gas but sometimes come across an electric oven and I am not always sure what temperature to put this on).

Temperature Guide:

Celsius (°C).	Fahrenheit (°F)	Gas Mark
70 °C	150°F	
80 °C	175 °F	
100 °C	200 °F	
110 °C	225 °F	1/4
120 °C	250 °F	1/2
140 °C	275 °F	1
150 °C	300 °F	2
160 °C	325 °F	3
180 °C	350 °F	4
190 °C	375 °F	5
200 °C	400 °F	6
220 °C	425 °F	7
230 °C	450 °F	8
240 °C	475 °F	9
260 °C	500 °F	9

All the jam recipes in this book are suitable for vegans and are gluten-free. Many of my family and friends are vegan or need a gluten-free diet and find it difficult to find products that are suitable for them, so made my own.

.

3 JAM RECIPES

Blueberry & Rhubarb Jam

This jam is one of my favourites and was invented by accident. While cooking blueberry jam, I found it easily became too thick and difficult to spread, so I decided to add rhubarb which gives this recipe a little bit of tartness and makes it easier to spread.

Ingredients:

1kg of blueberries
1kg of rhubarb
Juice of two lemon
 2kg of sugar

Method:

First you will need to chop the rhubarb into nice small chunks. Then give the rhubarb and berries good wash.

Place the rhubarb and blueberries into the jam preserving pan and cook for about five minutes. Mix the rhubarb and blueberries together until both have blended together for about 10 minutes.
Then add the lemon juice and then slowly add the sugar stirring constantly to stop the sugar from sticking to the bottom or crystallising. Continue on a rolling boil for about 15 minutes then check your jam in the usual way to see to if it is ready for setting and testing. Then retest.

When your jam is ready take off the heat, skim off any surface scum from the top of the jam, before pouring into hot sterilised jars using your funnel and then pop the lids on to stop contamination. Sterilisation process as previous pages.

Then allow the jam to cool before adding labels to ensure you know what the product is and what ingredients are in each jar. This jam can be kept for one year unopened. Once opened keep in the refrigerator for 4 to 6 weeks. Recipe will make around 14 small jars (180G)

Rhubarb and Ginger Jam

I love the woody taste that the ginger gives to the rhubarb and ginger jam.

Ingredients:

1 kg rhubarb
1 kg sugar
Juice of one Lemon
100g fresh root ginger (grated)

Tips:

✓ A great way to prepare your ginger is to use a small teaspoon and scrape this along your ginger. This method is a much easier way of peeling ginger, then just cut off any hard or dry bits with a knife. This will save you a lot of time.

Method:

Chop up the rhubarb into little chunks and give it a good wash. Then put the rhubarb into your preserve pan, on a low heat until the rhubarb begins to soften and breaks down. Once the rhubarb has softened, add the lemon juice, then stir in the sugar slowly to prevent the jam from burning or the sugar crystallising, then bring to a rolling boil. Then add fresh ginger to the other ingredients once it has come to the boil. If you put in the ginger too soon it can take the flavour of the ginger away.

Continue on a rolling boil for about 15 to 20 minutes then check your jam in the usual way to see to if it is ready for setting and testing. When your jam is ready take off the heat, skim off any surface scum from the top of the jam, pour into hot sterilised jars using your funnel and then pop the lids on to stop contamination.

Then when cool you can then label to ensure you know what the product is and what ingredients are in each jar. This jam can be kept for one year unopened. Once opened keep in the refrigerator for 4 to 6 weeks. Recipe will make around six small jars (180G)

Apple and Pineapple Jam

Ingredients:

2.75 kg Apples peeled and cored
750g Tinned or fresh pineapple chopped into cubes
Juice of 2 lemon
l litre pineapple juice
2.75 kg Sugar

Method:

Put all the cooking apples and lemon juice into the preserving pan. Then drain the syrup from the canned pineapple if using canned and make the juice up to 1 Litres (2pints).

Add the pineapple and the pineapple juice to the pan and then simply bring to the boil and simmer until the mixture turns into a pulp looking mixture. Then you are ready to add your sugar stir in the sugar well and bring to a rolling boil and simmer for about 15 minutes until it reaches setting point.

When your jam is ready take off the heat, skim off any surface scum for the top of the jam, pour into hot sterilised jars using your funnel and then pop the lids on to stop contamination.

Then allow the jam to cool, you can then label to ensure you know what the product is and what ingredients are in each jar. This jam can be kept for one year unopened. Once opened keep in the refrigerator for 4 to 6 weeks. Recipe will make around 24 small jars(180G)

Strawberry Jam

Tips:

- ✓ Strawberry jam is low in pectin and you might find it difficult to set, so use a natural Apple pectin which you can make yourself see previous instructions.
- ✓ Or you can use more Lemon juice in the jam, and I recommend 100 ml.
- ✓ Another way is to make your strawberry jam with another fruit that is high in pectin.
- ✓ You can also use a preservative sugar, but I find this is awfully expensive and not cost-effective.

Ingredients

1 kg strawberries
1 kg sugar
100 ml lemon Juice or
300 ml of natural Apple pectin optional

Method:

Wash the strawberries and place cut them up into half and place into your preserving pan. Slowly bring to the boil and lightly crush the strawberries using the back of a wooden spoon.

Then slowly add the sugar and stir until all the sugar has dissolved. The add the lemon juice. If you are going to use an Apple Pectin put in after the sugar, then turn up the heat and bring to a rolling boil. Cook for 20 minutes until the jam setting point but remember to remove from the heat whilst you test. See previous instructions for testing the setting point.

When your jam is ready take off the heat, skim off any surface scum for the top of the jam, pour into hot sterilised jars using your funnel and then pop the lids on to stop contamination.

Then allow the jam to cool then label to ensure you know what the product is and what ingredients are in each jar. This jam can be kept for one year unopened. Once opened keep in the refrigerator for 4 to 6 weeks. Recipe will make around six small jars(180G)

Strawberry and Prosecco Jam

Ingredients:

1kg Strawberries washed. Hulled and cut if large.
1kg Sugar or you can use jam sugar
100ml Lemon Juice
150 Prosecco

Method:

Put the strawberries into a large preserving pan and place over a low heat and simmer for approximately five minutes until soft. Then add the Prosecco and stir in.

Then add your sugar and stir until dissolved.Turn up the heat and bring to a rolling boil for approximately 15 to 20 minutes or until it reaches the setting point.

When your jam is ready take off the heat, skim off any surface scum for the top of the jam, pour into hot sterilised jars using your funnel and then pop the lids on to stop contamination.

Then allow to cool and then label to ensure you know what the product is and what ingredients are in each jar. This jam can be kept for one year unopened. Once opened keep in the refrigerator for 4 to 6 weeks. Recipe will make around six small jars(180G)

Blackberry Jam

Tips:

✓ You can use the juice of two lemons in your blackberry recipe if you wish but I think it is fine without.

Ingredients:

1 kg blackberries
1 kg of sugar
Juice of two lemons (optional)

Method:

Wash the blackberries and then drain and pat dry then place them in the preserving pan slowly bringing them to the boil and crush the blackberries with the back of a wooden spoon.

Slowly add the sugar to the mixture and let all the sugar dissolve before you bring to a rolling boil for around about 5 to 10 minutes until the jam setting point is reached, but remove from the heat whilst you test.

When your jam is ready take off the heat, skim off any surface scum for the top of the jam, pour into hot sterilised jars using your funnel and then pop the lids on to stop contamination.

Then allow the jam to cool and then label to ensure you know what the product is and what ingredients are in each jar. This jam can be kept for one year unopened. Once opened keep in the refrigerator for 4 to 6 weeks. Recipe will make around six small jars(180G)

Blackberry and Port Jam

This jam goes very well as a sauce with duck

Ingredients:

1kg Blackberries
1kg sugar
Juice of one lemon
150mls port

Method:

Wash the blackberries and then drain and pat dry and place in the preserving pan, slowly bringing them to the boil. Then crush the blackberries with the back of a wooden spoon.

Slowly add the sugar to the mixture and let all the sugar dissolve, add the lemon juice and bring to a rolling boil for around about 5 to 10 minutes until the jam reaches the setting point remove from the heat whilst you test.

When the jam has reached the setting point then add the port and just re-boil for two minutes to make sure that the jam is still at the point for set. But do not boil for too long or you will lose the taste of the port.

Then take off the heat, skim off any surface scum for the top of the jam, pour into hot sterilised jars using your funnel and then pop the lids on to stop contamination.

Allow the jam to go cool before you add labels to ensure you know what the product is and what ingredients are in each jar. This jam can be kept for one year unopened. Once opened keep in the refrigerator for 4 to 6 weeks. Recipe will make around six small jars(180G)

Mulled Wine Jam with Plums

Ingredients:

1.8 kg Red Plums barfed and stoned
1.8 kg Sugar
375g Mulled wine
Spice such as cinnamon, nutmeg, and cloves of your choice
A piece of orange zest from a quarter of orange without the white pith

Method:

Put the plums and the wine into the large preserving pan. Place the spices and orange zest into a piece of muslin, tie up and place in the pan. Bring to the boil and simmer gently for around about 20 minutes until the plums and skins are soft.

Remove the Muslin bag and add the sugar gently until it is all dissolved. Bring to a boil and then boil rapidly for about 10 minutes until the setting point is reached.

When your jam is ready take off the heat, skim off any surface scum for the top of the jam and pour into hot sterilised jars using your funnel and then pop the lids on to stop contamination.

Then allow the jam to cool and then label to ensure you know what the product is and what ingredients are in each jar. This jam can be kept for one year unopened. Once opened keep in the refrigerator for 4 to 6 weeks.

Damson Jam

Tips:

- ✓ Damsons are very much like plums, but they are much smaller and tarter and make a very lovely jam which sets very well. It has a lovely dark purple colour when cooking.
- ✓ Damsons can be quite fiddly to get the stones out of however I found the best way to do this is to squeeze the stones out.

Ingredients:

1 kg Damsons with stones out
Juice of one lemon
1 kg of sugar

Method:

You need to place all the damsons chopped in half into a large preserving pan with the lemon juice, but on a low heat until the damsons start to go soft and produce its own juice.

Add the sugar slowly and keep stirring until the sugar has all dissolved, add the lemon juice then bring to the boil and keep on a rolling boil for about 10 minutes until the jam reaches the setting point.

When your jam is ready take off the heat, skim off any surface scum from the top of the jam and pour into hot sterilised jars using your funnel and then pop the lids on to stop contamination.

Then once cool you can then label to ensure you know what the product is and what ingredients are in each jar. This jam can be kept for one year unopened. Once opened keep in the refrigerator for 4 to 6 weeks

Raspberry Jam

Ingredients:

1 kg raspberries
1 kg sugar
Juice of one lemon

Method:

Wash your raspberries then drain well and pop into your preserving pan and slowly bring to the boil. Slowly add the sugar to the mixture and let all the sugar dissolve, add the lemon juice, and bring to a rolling boil for around about 5 to 10 minutes until the jam setting point is reached. Remove from the heat whilst you test.

When your jam is ready take off the heat, skim off any surface scum from the top of the jam, pour into hot sterilised jars using your funnel and then pop the lids on to stop contamination.

Then allow the jam to cool and then label to ensure you know what the product is and what ingredients are in each jar. This jam can be kept for one year unopened. Once opened keep in the refrigerator for 4 to 6 weeks. Recipe will make around six small jars (180g)

Plum Jam

Plum jam goes very nicely with spareribs

Tips:
- ✓ To make Plum and Cinnamon Jam just add 2 tablespoons of powdered cinnamon after you have tested the jam and be sure to stir it in thoroughly so there is no powder on the surface.

Ingredients:

1 kg plums
1 kg sugar
juice of one lemon
2 tablespoons of powdered cinnamon

Method:

Give the plums a good wash, remove the stones and place the fruit into your preserving pan. Then put on a low heat and slowly begin to bring to the boil mashing the plums with the back of the wooden spoon.

Slowly add the sugar to the mixture and allow to dissolve then add the lemon juice and bring to a rolling boil for around about 5 to 10 minutes until the jam setting point is reached. Remove from the heat whilst you test. When your jam is ready take off the heat, skim off any surface scum from the top of the jam, pour into hot sterilised jars using your funnel and then pop the lids on to stop contamination.

When the jam is completely cool, you can then label to ensure you know what the product is and what ingredients are in each jar. This jam can be kept for one year unopened. Once opened keep in the refrigerator for 4 to 6 weeks. Recipe will make around six small jars(180G)

Cherry and Apple Jam

Ingredients:

1 kg sour apples
900ml pints water
1 kg cherries
 juice of one lemon
1.75kg sugar

Method:

Peel, core and slice the apples and place them into a large preserving pan with half a pint of water and simmer for 30 to 40 minutes until the apples are well stewed, then put into a jelly bag or muslin and leave to strain for several hours.

Put the apple extract which should be measured about 300g (10oz 1\2 pint) into a preserving pan with the cherries and lemon juice. Simmer gently for about 30 minutes, until most of the juice from the cherries has evaporated. Remove from the heat. Slowly add the sugar to the mixture and let all the sugar dissolve before bringing to a rolling boil for around about 10 minutes until the jam reaches setting point. Remove from the heat whilst you test. Add the powdered cinnamon after you have tested the jam and be sure to stir it in thoroughly so there is no powder on the surface.

When your jam is ready take off the heat, skim off any surface scum on the top, pour into hot sterilised jars using your funnel and then pop the lids on to stop contamination.

When cool, you can then label to ensure you know what the product is and what ingredients are in each jar. This jam can be kept for one year unopened. Once opened keep in the refrigerator for 4 to 6 weeks. Recipe will make around six small jars(180G)

4 MARMALADES

Orange Marmalade

Ingredients:

1.3 kg Oranges
2 Medium lemons
2.7 kg Granulated sugar

Method:

Wash the oranges and lemons thoroughly and dry them. Cut the oranges and lemons in half and squeeze all the juice - you should get around about 500 ml (1 pint). Then remove all the pith from the oranges and put this into a muslin with the lemon flesh, rind, and pips. Then cut the orange peel into thin shreds or thicker pieces if you prefer. Place them into a large preserving pan with the orange juice, the bag of muslin and 2.8ltr (5pint) of water.

Bring to the boil and then simmer gently for two hours until the contents of the pan reduces by Half and the peel has softened. Then remove the muslin bag and place in a strainer over the top of the pan for half an hour so the juices can run from the muslin. You can give this a bit of a squeeze if you like. The liquid from the muslin contains the pectin which helps the marmalade have a good set.

Slowly add the sugar and stir until completely dissolved. Bring to a rolling boil for about 20 minutes, until the setting point is reached. Remove from the heat to check the setting point and if it is not set pop back on the heat for another five minutes and check again.
Then remove all the scum from the top of the marmalade and allow this to cool, I personally find that if you jar the marmalade too early all the peel will float to the top, a lot of books recommend leaving it for 10 minutes, but I recommend leaving it a good half an hour then you can be assured that the peel will not float to the top. The marmalade will still be extremely hot after a half an hour. Then pour your mixture into warm sterilised jars and put the lids on straightaway.
After cooling completely, label and store. You can store these for around about one year unopened, when opened refrigerate and eat within 4 to 6 weeks. This will make approximately 17 jars of about 190g

Lemon Marmalade

Ingredients:

1.3 kg unwaxed lemons
2.8ltr Water
2.7 kg Granulated sugar

Method:

You need to wash the lemons thoroughly and dry them. Cut the lemons in half and squeeze all the juice from them. You should get around about 500 ml (1 pint). Then remove all the pith from the lemons and put this into a muslin, along with all the pips and bits of lemon that came out when squeezing the lemon. Then you need to cut the peel into thin shreds or corse ones if you prefer. Place into a large preserving pan with the juice, the muslin Bag and 2.8ltr (5pint) of water.

Bring to the boil and then simmer gently for two hours until the contents of the pan reduces by Half and the peel has softened. Then remove the muslin bag and place in a strainer over the top of the pan for half an hour so the juices can run from the muslin. You can give this a bit of a squeeze if you like. The liquid from the muslin contains the pectin which helps the marmalade have a good set.

Then slowly add the sugar and stir until completely dissolved. Bring to a rolling boil for about 20 minutes until the setting point is reached. Remove from the heat to check the setting point if it is not set pop back on for another five minutes and check again.

Then remove all the scum from the top of the marmalade, allow the marmalade to cool, I personally find that if you jar the marmalade too early all the peel floats to the top, a lot of books recommend leaving it 10 minutes, but I recommend leaving it a good half an hour then you can be assured that the peel will not float to the top. The marmalade will still be extremely hot after a half an hour. Then pour your mixture into warm sterilised jars and put the lids on.

Allow to cool and then label, you can store these for around about one year unopened. When opened refrigerate and eat within 4 to 6 weeks. This will make approximately 17 jars of about 190g

Clementine and Other Flavoured Marmalade

Tips:

✓ To make a whiskey marmalade or gin marmalade just add 2 to 4 tablespoons of the required alcohol.

✓ To make ginger marmalade, grate fresh ginger about 100 g and then put it in the pan at the same time as the sugar and that will make a lovely warming ginger marmalade.

✓ you could chop all the clementines in a processor using the post button until they are shredded, but not turned to mush

Recipe for Clementine Whiskey Marmalade
Ingredients:

900g Clementines scrubbed rinsed and halved with pips removed.
Juice of two lemons
900g Granulated sugar
2 to 3 tablespoons of whiskey or you can use brandy if you prefer.

Method:

Squeeze all the juice from the clementines and then finely shred the skin with a sharp knife. Put all the chopped fruit into a large preserving pan and pour in 900ml or 1 ½ pints of water and bring to the boil. Then reduce to a simmer and cook gently for 30 minutes or longer until the peel has softened.

Then add the lemon juice and stir in well. Add the sugar slowly stirring in thoroughly until all the sugar has dissolved, then bring to a rolling boil for about 25 minutes or until the marmalade reaches the setting point. Remove from the heat to check the setting point if it is not set pop back on for another five minutes and check again.

Then remove all the scum from the top of the marmalade and allow this to cool for around about half an hour. Then you will need to stir the whiskey into the marmalade just before jarring. Then pour your mixture into warm sterilised jars and put the lids on. Allow to cool and then label. Store these for around about one year unopened when opened refrigerate and eat within 4 to 6 weeks. This will make approximately 8 jars of about 190g

5 FRUIT CURDS

Fruit Curds Explained

Curds are a creamy fruit mixture which is made with fruit, eggs, butter, and sugar. Curds have a short shelf Life due to the eggs in the mixture but can be frozen to extend the life. Curds are best made in small quantities and put into small jars, for storing in the cupboard up to 3 months.

You can freeze in small freezer containers for up to 6 months. Curds should be cooked in a double pan.

- ✓ **A double pan is a traditional British a cooking utensil consisting of two saucepans, one fitting inside the other. The bottom saucepan contains water that, while boiling, gently heats food in the upper pan. Americans and Canadians call this a double boiler.**
- ✓ **You can use a very good non-stick normal pan (small), but this does create more work, as you will need to constantly stir the curd to prevent burning.**
- ✓ **It is important not to be distracted at this point, because if the curd burns, it will have to be discarded and all your hard work and expense is wasted. This tip comes from personal experience!**

The cooking heat should be at a low temperature. Curds should be continuously stirred during cooking and will be creamy and coat the back of the spoon when ready and will thicken as they cool.

Curds can be used as a nice treat to put in a cake as a filling, a spread or maybe to use as a source for ice cream or puddings or even in a yoghurt.

Lemon Curd

Ingredients:

4 large unwaxed lemons
450g Sugar
150g unsalted Butter
4 large eggs

Method:

Wash the lemons and fine grate the lemon peel. Then cut the lemon in half and squeeze all the juice out of the lemons. whisk your eggs up in a dish ready to use. Then put the butter into the saucepan, melt gently, then add the sugar, lemon juice and the peel. When the sugar has all dissolved, add the well beaten egg and keep stirring. Once it starts to boil, turn to a lower heat, and keep stirring for 6 to 8 minutes until the mixture is nice and thick.

When your curd is ready take off the heat and pour into hot sterilised jars using your funnel and then pop the lids on to stop contamination. Or you can cool the mixture and pour into small freezing containers. You only get four small jars 190g

Then allow to cool and label to ensure you know what the product is and what ingredients are in it. This can be kept for 3 months unopened. Once opened keep in the refrigerator for 7 days.

Orange Curd

Ingredients:

2 or 3 oranges
450 g of sugar
150 g unsalted butter
4 large eggs

Method:

Wash the Orange and finely grate the orange peel Then cut the oranges in half and squeeze all the juice out of the orange. Whisk your eggs up in a dish ready to use. Then put the butter into the saucepan to melt, before adding the sugar, orange juice and the peel. When the sugar has all dissolved then you can add the well beaten egg and keep stirring the mixture all the time. Once it starts to boil, turn to a lower heat, and keep stirring for 6 to 8 minutes until the mixture is nice and thick.

When your curd is ready take off the heat and pour into hot sterilised jars using your funnel and then pop the lids on to stop contamination. Or you can cool the mixture and pour into small freezing containers. You only get four small jars 190g

Then allow to cool and label to ensure you know what the product is and what ingredients are in it. This can be kept for 3 months unopened. Once opened keep in the refrigerator for 7 days.

Lime Curd

Ingredients:

6 limes
450g sugar
150g butter
4 large eggs

Method:

Wash the limes and finely grate the peel. Then cut the limes in half and squeeze all the juice out and retain. Whisk your eggs up in a dish ready to use. Then put the butter into the saucepan to melt, then add the sugar, lime juice and the peel. When the sugar has all dissolved then you can add the well beaten egg. Stirring the mixture all the time, once it starts to boil, turn to a lower heat, and keep stirring for 6 to 8 minutes until the mixture is nice and thick.

When your curd is ready take off the heat and pour into hot sterilised jars using your funnel and then pop the lids on to stop contamination. Or you can cool the mixture and pour into small freezing containers. You only get four small jars 190g

Then allow to cool and label to ensure you know what the product is and what ingredients are in it. This can be kept for 3 months unopened. Once opened keep in the refrigerator for 7 days.

6 CHUTNEY

How To Test Your Chutney Is Ready

Finding the setting point for chutneys:

You will know when the chutney is ready by using a wooden spoon to drag a channel through the chutney so that you can see the bottom of the pan in the gap.

If the channel fills immediately with liquid, then it is not ready. So, cook for another 10 minutes and recheck again.

The chutney is ready once the channel does not fill immediately with liquid and the mixture has become thick and glutinous.

Do this when cooking any of the following chutney recipes

Patricia's Home-made Piccalilli

Ingredients:

450g (1lb) Onions chopped in chugs
1 Big Cauliflower chopped into florets
900g mixed vegetables diced or cut you can choose from:
Cucumber, French/runner beans, Courgettes, green tomatoes, even carrots
3 large cloves of garlic, crushed
1.4ltr White Malt Vinegar
100g Corn Flour
450g Granulated Sugar
50g Mustard Powder
25g Turmeric Powder
I tsp Salt

Tips:
- ✓ To make the piccalilli totally gluten free, replace the white malt vinegar with cider vinegar. Some people are more sensitive to gluten and this can include malt vinegar.
- ✓ Use a glass bowl as a plastic bowl will stain yellow.
- ✓ To make chilli piccalilli add 3-4 chillies to the mix.

Method:
Wash all the vegetables thoroughly, then put all the vegetables with the garlic, sugar and salt into a large preserving pan with 1.1ltr of the vinegar (the rest of the vinegar is for mixing the sauce, which will be added later. Bring the ingredients to the boil and then simmer for 10 minutes.

Meanwhile make the sauce in a medium glass bowl like this: Sieve the corn flour, mustard powder and turmeric powder into the bowl and mix, pour in the vinegar slowly to prevent lumps and achieve a nice paste. Then add this to the cooked vegetables slowly, stirring as you go to prevent lumps. Simmer for about 5 minutes, stirring constantly to prevent lumps and the piccalilli from sticking to the bottom of the pan.

Turn off the heat and carefully pour into hot sterilised jars using your funnel and pop on the lids to stop contamination. Sterilisation process as previously described. Cool and label as before and store in a cool place for at least 2 weeks before using, the longer it is stored the more it will mature. You can keep it up to a year. Once open refrigerate and eat within 5 to 6 weeks

Thai Chutney

This recipe is gluten-free. I came up with this recipe when I was travelling in Thailand last winter and decided to have a go at cooking with their ingredients whilst out there, I hope you enjoy this recipe.

Ingredients:

1kg mango
300g pineapple
200g soft light sugar
100g chopped or grated Ginger
250mls of cider vinegar
3tbls fresh chilies (or you can use dried)
One larger onion chopped
Half teaspoon Lemongrass

Tips:
✓ The best way the peel the ginger is to use a teaspoon and scrape the skin off and then rough trim with knife.

Method:

Peel and chop the mango and the pineapple into small cubes then wash thoroughly and put the mango, pineapple, onion, sugar, vinegar, chillies, and ginger into a large chutney pan or preserving pan. Chutney does splash when boiling so you need a big pan to avoid a splashed kitchen. It can also deliver a nasty burn if it splashes you, so take care.

Bring to the boil then simmer, keep stirring the chutney every now and then. Towards the end of the cooking, stir more frequently to prevent the chutney from sticking to the bottom of the pan and burning. Testing as previously described. When cooked turn off the heat and leave to stand for 5 minutes.

Then carefully jar into warm sterilised jars using your funnel. This recipe will make around about 6 to 7 small jars of chutney (180g)
Then once cool you can add labels to ensure you know what the product is and what ingredients are in each jar. This chutney can be kept for one year unopened. Once opened keep in the refrigerator for 4 to 6 weeks.

Vintage English Apple Chutney

✓ This chutney will go very nicely with any cheeseboard or cold meats

Ingredients:

Three medium onions chopped
1 kg of English cooking apples
125 g of sultanas
1tbsp of ground coriander
1tbsp of paprika
1tbsp of mixed spice
Half tbsp of salt
350 g of granulated sugar
700 mils of malt vinegar

Method:

Pop all the ingredients into a large chutney pan and bring to the boil. Staring frequently until all the sugar has completely. Then turn down the heat and simmer for around about 1 hour stirring from time to time to stop the chutney from sticking to the bottom of the pan and burning. After about 1 hour start checking that the chutney is ready. (See previous instructions)

If the chutney is not quite ready cook for around another 10 minutes and check again, continue in this way until your chutney has fully cooked. Then carefully pour into your sterilised jars using your funnel and pop on sterilised lids to prevent contamination. and leave to cool. The sterilisation process is described at the start of the book.

Then label your chutney and store for about two months before eating. It can be kept unopened for up to 1 year, but once opened keep the chutney in the refrigerator and consume within 4 to 5 weeks.

Gluten Free Spicy Beetroot and Apple Chutney

This is a favourite chutney of mine to cook and it is great to have any time of the year but especially at Christmas time, and is perfect with cold meats, cheese, and a pork pie. Great in a ham sandwich too…

Tips:

✓ An easy way to prepare the ginger is to use a small teaspoon and scrape this along the skin. A much easier way of peeling the ginger, then just cut off any hard or dry bits with a knife. This will save you a lot of time.

✓ This recipe is gluten-free because it uses red wine vinegar instead of malt vinegar.

Ingredients:

1 kg beetroot peeled and diced into small chunks
3 large cooking apples peeled, cored, and chopped into chunks
2 large onions finely chopped
600ml red wine vinegar
600g granulated sugar
150g fresh root ginger
1 tbsp coriander seeds
2 tsp allspice berries
1 tsp caraway seeds
3 tsp dried chilli flakes or you can use fresh chilies
2 tsp salt

Method:

Add the apple, beetroot onion, red wine vinegar and sugar into the preserving pan and begin to a boil. Meanwhile take your coriander seeds, caraway seeds, allspice berries, and pop them into a pestle and mortar and grind them up. Then add these to the pan along with the chilies, salt, and the grated root ginger. Stir all the ingredients together well then bring to the boil and simmer for around about one hour. Stirring regularly. Test when you think the chutney is ready.

If the chutney is not quite ready cook for around another 10 minutes and check again, continue in this way until your chutney has fully cooked. Then carefully pour into your sterilised jars using your funnel and pop on sterilised lids to prevent contamination. and leave to cool. The sterilisation process is described at the start of the book.

Then label your chutney and store for about two months before eating. It can be kept unopened for up to 1 year, but once opened keep the chutney in the refrigerator and consume within 4 to 5 weeks. This recipe will make approximately 14 small jars (180g)

Plum and Cranberry Chutney - Gluten Free

This recipe uses red wine vinegar instead of malt vinegar, which makes it gluten-free

Ingredients:

2 large onions chopped
1lk plums stoned and chopped
100g Cranberries chopped
300 g Cooking apples
1tbsp finely grated ginger or you can use powdered, but I think fresh is better.
1 tbsp black mustard seed
1 tbsp ground cumin
1 tbsp paprika
I tsp fresh chilli or chilli flakes
400 ml red wine vinegar
500g light muscovado sugar

Method:

Add all the in the ingredients in the to the preserving pan except the sugar. Bring to the boil slowly, then reduce the heat and simmer for 10 minutes until the plums are tender.

Then proceed to stir in the sugar and add 1 tablespoon of salt keep stirring until all the sugar has dissolved and cook for 20 to 30 minutes stirring occasionally to prevent it sticking to the bottom. Do this until the mixture looks thick and pulpy and then test for setting as described.

Then carefully pour into your sterilised jars using your funnel and pop on sterilised lids to prevent contamination. and leave to cool. The sterilisation process is described at the start of the book.
Then label your chutney and store for at least two weeks before eating. It can be kept unopened for up to 1 year in a cool dark place, but once opened keep the chutney in the refrigerator and consume within 4 to 5 weeks.

Caramelised Onion Chutney

✓ This chutney goes very well with cheese on a Ploughman's lunch or on a cheese sandwich.

Ingredients:

1.5 kg of onions
3 tbsp olive oil or oil of your choice
250 g Dark muscovado sugar
200 ml Malt vinegar
4 Cloves of garlic crushed
3 tbsp Whole-grain mustard
1 tsp Salt
1 tsp Paprika

Method:

Peel and slice the onions very thinly. Then gently heat the oil in the preserving pan and put the onions in to start softening and to start caramelising them, stir occasionally to stop them from burning. Stir in 3 tablespoons of sugar and turn up the heat so the onions caramelise and turn rich golden brown but do not let them burn, add the rest of the sugar then the rest of the ingredients.

Cook for approximately 15 minutes until the mixture becomes thick.

To see the setting process, see the page before the chutneys Then take off the heat and jar into hot sterile jars and put the lid on straight away to prevent contamination.
Leave to cool, label, and leave to mature for a couple of weeks before it consuming as this will make the product taste nicer and allow the flavours to come out. You can keep these for approximately one year but will keep in the refrigerator for 4 to 6 weeks.

Pear Chutney – Gluten Free

This recipe is gluten-free as it uses cider vinegar instead of malt vinegar, which contains gluten. This chutney is great for windfalls or unripe pears, and tastes wonderful served with cheese, cold ham, or savoury tarts

Ingredients:

750 g of pears peeled cored and cut in to approximately 2cm squares
350 g of onions chopped
350 g of red or green tomatoes sliced
125 g of raisins or sultanas chopped
Three peppercorns crushed
350 g Demerara sugar
1 tsp Cayenne pepper
1 tsp ground ginger or freshly grated ginger which I prefer
1 tsp sea salt or salt
450 mL of cider vinegar

Method:

Put all the ingredients into a large preserving pan bring to the boil slowly dissolving all the sugar. Then reduce the heat and simmer gently, uncovered, for approximately two hours until the mixture thickens and takes on a dark caramelised appearance.

To check the setting process, follow previous instruction at the start of the Chutneys. Then take off the heat and jar into hot sterile jars and put the lid on straight away to prevent contamination.
Leave to cool, label, and leave to mature for a couple of weeks before it consuming as this will make the product taste nicer and allow the flavours to come out. You can keep these for approximately one year but will keep in the refrigerator for 4 to 6 weeks.

Pickled Red Cabbage – Gluten Free

This recipe uses white wine vinegar which is gluten-free instead of malt vinegar, which contains small traces of gluten.

Ingredients:

I large red cabbage
3 tbsp Salt
1.lts white Wine vinegar
125g light muscovado sugar or use white sugar
1tbsp black pepper seeds
1tbsp Coriander seeds

Method:

You will need to take the outer leaves of the cabbage off and then cut the cabbage in half and take out the core then cut them in quarters and slice into shreds. Then place into a large bowl and mix with the salt and leave overnight to drain in the sieve with a tea towel over the top.

In the interim you can prepare the vinegar you will need to put all the vinegar in a large bowl with the black pepper seeds and Coriander seeds and the sugar and stir until all the sugar has dissolved and cover with some cling film and leave until the cabbage is ready to jar.

Rinse off the salt from the cabbage and then place into a clean dry tea-towel, to remove excess water and leave for 10 minutes wrapped up in the towel to dry.
Put cabbage into hot sterilised jars using a pair of tongs. Then add the vinegar mixture using a Glass jug and then put on the lids. The pickled cabbage is then ready to label.

Store in a dark cold place to mature for one month to allow the flavours to develop and mellow once opened keep in the refrigerator. You can keep this unopened for a year and the recipe will make approximately six largish jars (pasta sauce size).

Pickled Onions

Tip:

✓ If you would like to make this recipe into a gluten-free pickled onion recipe you can use cider vinegar I find it works quite well and it is great for people that can't have gluten.

Ingredients:

250g salt table or rock salt
5lk Pickling onions or shallots, peeled and trimmed
2ltrs Malt vinegar
200g light muscovado Sugar
4 tbsp mixed packaging spices or you can make you own with the following

Or

1 tbsp of each: Coriander seeds, allspice, juniper berries, black peppercorns, black mustard seeds and one cinnamon stick and 3 or 4 Bay leaves

Method:

Peel the onions wash under cool water, then put into a large bowl with the salt to soak overnight.

Meanwhile start preparing your vinegar mixture by pouring all the vinegar into a large pan adding all your spices, the bay leaves, and the sugar to the vinegar. Bring this vinegar mixture to boil until all the sugar has dissolved and then allow to cool.

Then drain the onions and give a quick rinse and put them into a strainer to drain. Then put the onions into cold sterilised jars, pour in the vinegar mixture and seal with a sterilised lid. Store for at least three weeks before using. Will keep well for a year but once open refrigerate and eat within 3 to 6 weeks.

Chilli Jelly

Tips:

- ✓ There are two ways that you can make chilli jelly; first I will give you the original way. Then I will give you the second way that I make it, which is very much a way of using all the bits that you think you would throw away. This will help to save money.
- ✓ Can also use the jelly to make other types of jellies like mint jelly or rosemary jelly.

Ingredients:

675g Cooking apples
Approx. 675g Sugar
Juice of 1 lemon
2-3 tsp chilli flakes
(this depends on how hot you require it, add more chilli flakes to your desired heat level)

Method:

Put the chopped apples including all the cores, pips and skin into the preserving pan and add 1.7 litres (3 pints) of cold water and bring to the boil and simmer for approximately 40 minutes until the apples are all mushy and completely stewed down. Mash them a little with a potato masher or a fork.
Pour the mixture into a jelly bag or muslin sieve set over a large bowl leaving the juice to dry naturally overnight. Do not be tempted to squeeze the pulp mixture if you want a clear liquid.

Then measure the juice for every 500 ml / 1pint of juice you will need 450g (1lb) of sugar. Pour the clear juice into your large serving pan bring to the boil then add the sugar and lemon juice. Stir until all the sugar has dissolved and bring to a rolling boil for 20 to 30 minutes or until the jelly reaches the setting point then remove from the heat to test the setting point, (as explained earlier in the book). When your jelly is ready take off the heat, skim off any surface scum for the top and then leave the mixture to cool for approximately 10 minutes, before stirring in the chilli flakes.

Pour into hot sterilised jars using your funnel and then pop the lids on to stop contamination.

Then allow the jelly to cool completely before you label to ensure you know what the product is and what ingredients are in the jar. This can be stored for one year unopened. Once opened keep in the refrigerator for 4 to 6 weeks. Recipe will make around six small jars(180g)

My Way of Making Chilli Jelly

Chilli Jelly goes nicely with cheese, on cold meats, pork chops or with salmon

Ingredients:

Use all the leftover Apple peel, core, pips, and the skins of any lemons after removing the juice. When I am doing a big cook, I do not throw them away. I use them to make chilli jelly

Method:

Put everything; the apple peel, core, pips and lemon skins in a large pan and cover them with water, bring to the boil, turn the heat down and continue to simmer for approximately 40 to 45 minutes, with the lid on. Then I allow it to cool for a while, before putting the mixture through a muslin and allow it to drain overnight.

Then you will get a nice syrup liquid which you can measure out, for every 500ml (1 pint) you will need 450 g (1 lb) of sugar. Pour the liquid into your preserving pan and slowly bring to the boil, add in the sugar slowly, then bring to a rolling boil. Whilst it is boiling a scum will form on top of the mixture. It will take approximately 20 minutes to reach setting point for a jelly. Turn off the heat and test in the same way as you would for a jam.

When your jelly is ready take off the heat, skim off any surface scum from the top of the jelly, Leave the mixture to cool for approximately 10 to 15 minutes, then stir in the chilli flakes.

If you do not let the jelly cool before putting in the chilli flakes, they will just float to the top of the jelly. Then pour into hot sterilised jars using your funnel and then pop the lids on to stop contamination.

Allow the jelly to cool before labelling to ensure you know what the product is and what ingredients are in each jar. This jelly can be kept for one year unopened. Once opened keep in the refrigerator for 4 to 6 weeks. Recipe will make around six small jars(180g)

ABOUT THE AUTHOR

Patricia originally came from Lowestoft in Suffolk, but now lives in
Derbyshire and has three grown up children and eight lovely grand children
She makes regular appearances at Long Eaton Market, Tansley Market,
Ilkeston Market, and many of the big summer shows and fairs.
She is available to book a table display at Fetes, Fairs and Food Markets.

You can follow her on Facebook and on Twitter or send an email to:
triciasweet58@gmail.com
Or phone: 07469211162

The following blank pages are for you to add your own recipes, notes and inspirations this book may give you.

If you would like to try out any of these preserves, please visit my Etsy shop:

www.etsy.com/uk/shop/pattriciasjams

Old Dower House
Chutney

Printed in Great Britain
by Amazon

67715388R00041